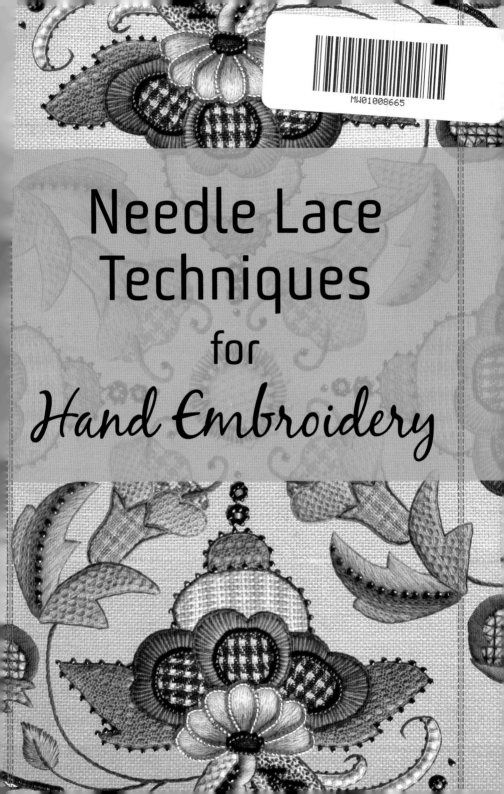

Needle Lace Techniques

for

Hand Embroidery

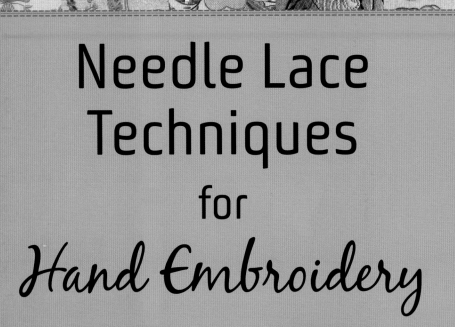

Needle Lace
Techniques
for
Hand Embroidery

Hazel Blomkamp

SEARCH PRESS

CONTENTS

This edition published in 2017

Search Press Limited
Wellwood, North Farm Road,
Tunbridge Wells, Kent TN2 3DR

First published in South Africa
by Hazel Blomkamp, 2015

Text copyright © Hazel Blomkamp, 2017

Illustrations and photography copyright
© Hazel Blomkamp and Darren Wilson, 2017

Design copyright © Search Press Ltd. 2017

The techniques in this booklet have been tweaked and
adapted to use as stitches to enhance the art of hand
embroidery. It is not intended that the book should be of
use to lace makers.

The techniques in the numbered needle lace section
have been based on the numbers provided in the DMC
Library Encyclopedia of Needlework by T.H. de Dillmont.

ISBN: 978-1-78221-518-9

The Publishers and author can accept no responsibility
for any consequences arising from the information,
advice or instructions given in this publication.

Suppliers

If you have difficulty in obtaining any of the materials
and equipment mentioned in this book, then please visit
the Search Press website for details of suppliers:
www.searchpress.com

See more designs on the author's website:
www.hazelblomkamp.co.za

Printed in China through Asia Pacific Offset

BASIC KNOWLEDGE AND TIPS

- Each needle lace technique is on a separate page (or pages). By slipping a magnetic cross-stitch board under the page, you can use the magnetic rulers that come with the board to mark the row that you are working on, making these instructions easier to follow.

- For ease, diagrams of the techniques are depicted on square blocks.

- If you are new to needle lace techniques, test them initially on a scrap of fabric.

- Work in square blocks first, using a Perle No. 12, or even a Perle No. 8 thread. This gives you the opportunity to familiarise yourself with the techniques, and to get a feel for your stitching tension before you move on to filling the shapes.

- When you feel more confident, draw some simple shapes onto a scrap of fabric and apply the techniques to these designs, increasing and decreasing as necessary to fill the shapes.

- Once you begin to work on your embroidery pieces, Cordonnet No. 80/No. 40, or Perle No. 16/Perle No. 12 tatting thread are the best thread types to use.

- It is almost impossible to create a smooth edge to your needle lace. Try to be as even and smooth as you can, but be aware that you will need to either outline the area or cover the edge in some way. Crewel stitches or beads are suitable for this task. *For alternative method turn to page 13.*

- Always work with your fabric stretched taut in a hoop to prevent puckering.

- Use a size 7/8 embroidery needle to work the backstitches (BS) and a size 26/28 tapestry (blunt-end) needle to work the detached buttonhole stitches (DBH). *For more detail on these stitches, turn to page 11.*

- Each shape that you wish to fill with needle lace should be surrounded with BS. Use these stitches to anchor the lace.

- Don't expect your BS to be perfect – it's not a perfect world. Use them as a guide and an anchor only. Adjust your tension and counting to suit the DBH, not the BS.

- The majority of needle lace techniques use DBH.

Important note on Numbered Stitches

The techniques in the numbered needle lace section (pages 6–30) have been based on the numbers provided in the DMC Library Encyclopedia of Needlework by Thérèse de Dillmont. **Whilst it might appear that some stitches are missing** (such as Stitch No. 12), this is because they were not suitable for use in this particular area of embroidery; thus, they have been deliberately excluded.

HOW TO READ THE PATTERNS

- Each instruction notes the length of the backstitches (BS) in the top row.

- With the exception of those stitches in the Edges section (pages 75–105), it usually doesn't matter which direction you choose to stitch your needle lace. You make life easier for yourself if you choose to work the first row on the edge that will give you the longest and straightest row, decreasing or increasing from there.

- To start the first row, come up at the side, approximately level with where the ridge of the detached buttonhole (DBH) will lie. Alternatively, depending on where you have chosen to start, glide in as smoothly as you can from the BS curve.

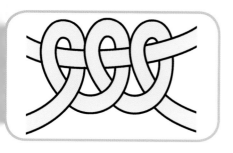

- A 'group' means two or more DBH that lie together, usually preceded and followed by a gap, or loop.

- A 'loop' means a single strand, leading up to or away from either a single DBH or a group of buttonhole stitches, as described above.

- 'LR' means working from left to right; 'RL' means working from right to left.

- Refer to the basic stitches section on pages 11–13 for instructions on how to finish off a section of needle lace by attaching it to the BS at the bottom.

- Always make sure that the beginning and end of each row are approximately level with one another.

- When working further down, always make sure that you space your rows so that the sides of the needle lace are neither bunching up, nor stretching down too far. If you are unsure of where to come up at the beginning of a row, pull the middle section of the row you have just completed down with the point of your needle, see how far it stretches, then come up for the start of your row approximately level with that point.

BASIC STITCHES

Backstitch (BS)

Working from right to left, bring the needle up a stitch length before the end of the line you wish to stitch. Go in at the end of the line, coming up again a stitch length away from the beginning of the stitch you are working. Repeat as necessary, keeping your stitch length as even as possible.

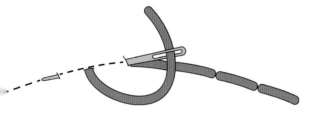

Detached buttonhole stitch (DBH)

Surround the area that you intend to fill with small BS, which will be what you use to anchor the detached buttonhole stitch. Bring your needle up on the side, as indicated in the diagram, go over and under the first horizontal BS and, making sure that the working thread is under the needle, pull through to form a buttonhole stitch. Snake through the vertical BS at the end of the row. The second and subsequent rows are anchored in the loops between the stitches.

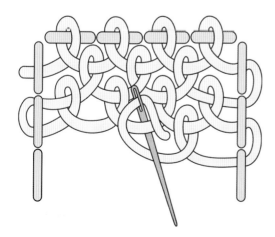

Needle lace bottom row

Continue working the DBH until you reach the bottom of the section that you intend to fill. It does not matter whether you are working a right to left (RL), or left to right (LR) row. For the purposes of these instructions, assume you have worked a LR row to correspond with the diagram below.

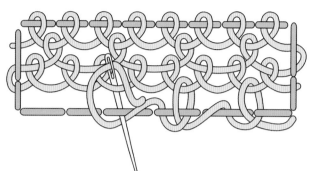

» **1** At the end of the row, instead of snaking through the BS, take the needle through the fabric to the other side.

» **2** Bring the needle up directly below the BS at the bottom, just in from the corner on the right.

» **3** The last row continues the pattern of the technique and attaches the needle lace to the BS at the same time.

» **4** Depending on how far you need to travel to make the first buttonhole stitch in the pattern you may need to whip the first BS, so that the loop – which would otherwise form – becomes lost. In the diagram above, this has not been necessary.

» **5** Working from right to left, form the DBH which goes through the loop, pushing the needle through the BS and the loop in the previous row at the same time. Make sure that the working thread is below the tip of the needle.

» **6** Pull the needle through to form the DBH, making sure that the lace pulls down and stretches over the shape that you have covered.

» **7** Whip the next BS to lose the loop and create the next DBH.

» **8** Continue in this way until you reach the left corner. The needle lace should be attached and evenly stretched over the entire section.

» **9** Take your needle through the fabric to end off at the back.

Alternative method

Only anchor the needle lace to the BS in the top row, going into and coming out of the fabric at the sides and the bottom. Thereafter, whip the surrounding BS to create a fine, neat edge as indicated in this diagram. Whip the top row after each needle lace group.

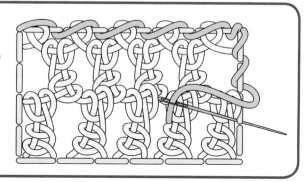

THE
STITCHES

NUMBERED STITCHES

STITCH NO. 1

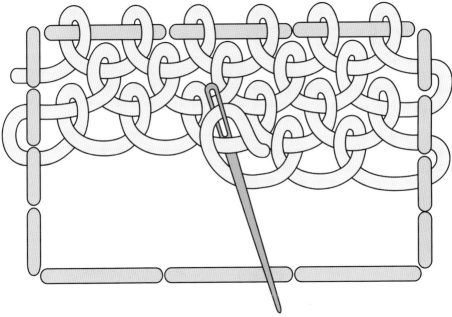

PREPARATION	TOP ROW STITCH LENGTH
BS outline	To accommodate 2 x DBH

» **1** Working LR, 2 x DBH into every BS along the top. Go through the nearest BS down the right-hand side that is level with the ridge of the DBH in the row you have just worked. Snake down through the next BS.

» **2** Working RL, 1 x DBH into each gap between the DBH in the previous row, until you reach the end of the row. Snake down to start the next row.

» **3** Keep working rows in this way until you have filled the required space. Following the instructions for the bottom row (see page 13), attach the DBH to the BS at the bottom.

STITCH NO. 1 (CORDED)

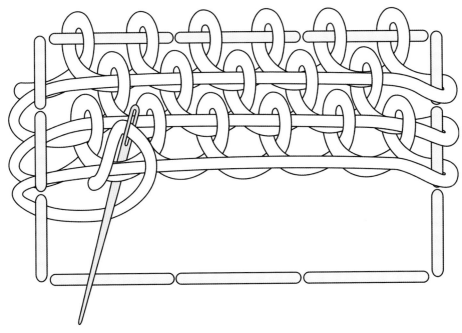

PREPARATION	TOP ROW STITCH LENGTH
BS outline	To accommodate 2 x DBH

» **1** Working LR, 2 x DBH into every BS along the top. Go through the nearest BS down the right-hand side that is level with the ridge of the DBH in the row you have just worked. Take your thread back to the left side and go under the nearest BS. Snake down through the next BS.

» **2** Working LR, 1 x DBH into each gap between the DBH in the previous row, taking in the thread (or cord) that you created at the end of the last row. Take your thread back to the left side and go under the nearest BS. Snake down through the next BS.

» **3** Keep working rows in this way until you have filled the required space. It is important to note that this technique does not stretch; taking this into account, you should adjust the tension of the DBH accordingly.

» **4** Following the instructions for the bottom row (see page 13) and working from RL, attach the DBH to the BS at the bottom. There is no cord to incorporate into the row as you do not need to create one.

STITCH NO. 2

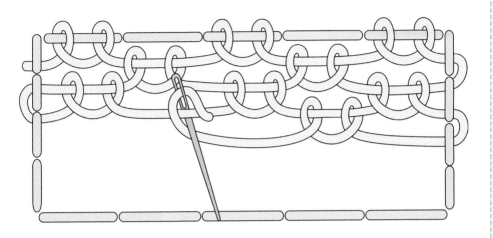

PREPARATION	TOP ROW STITCH LENGTH
BS outline	To accommodate 2 x DBH

» **1** Working LR, [2 x DBH into first BS, miss a BS]; repeat [--] to end. Go through the nearest BS down the right-hand side that is level with the ridge of the DBH in the row you have just worked. Snake down through the next BS.

» **2** Working RL, 2 x DBH into each loop. Go through the nearest BS down the left-hand side that is level with the ridge of the DBH in the row you have just worked. Snake down to the next row.

» **3** Keep working rows in this way until you have filled the required space. Following the instructions for the bottom row (see page 13), attach the DBH to the BS at the bottom.

STITCH NO. 3

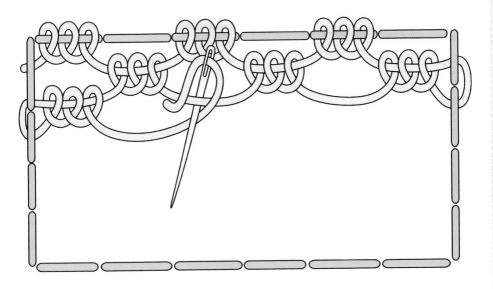

PREPARATION	TOP ROW STITCH LENGTH
BS outline	To accommodate 3 x DBH

» **1** Working LR, [3 x DBH into first BS, miss a BS]; repeat [--] to end. Go through the nearest BS down the right-hand side that is level with the ridge of the DBH in the row you have just worked. Snake down through the next BS.

» **2** Working RL, 3 x DBH into each loop. Go through the nearest BS down the left-hand side that is level with the ridge of the DBH in the row you have just worked. Snake down to the next row.

» **3** Keep working rows in this way until you have filled the required space. Following the instructions for the bottom row (see page 13), attach the DBH to the BS at the bottom.

STITCH NO. 4

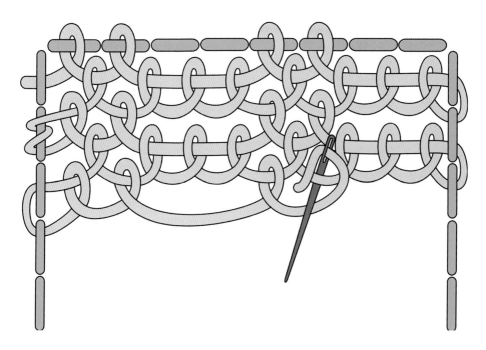

PREPARATION	TOP ROW STITCH LENGTH
BS outline	To accommodate 1 x DBH

» **1** Working LR, [1 x DBH into BS, 1 x DBH into BS, miss 2 BS]; repeat [--] to end. Go through the nearest BS down the right-hand side that is level with the ridge of the DBH in the row you have just worked. Snake down through the next DS.

» **2** *Working RL, [3 x DBH into large loop, 1 x DBH into small loop]; repeat [--] to end. Snake down through the next BS.

» **3** Working LR, [1 x DBH into first loop, 1 x DBH into next loop, miss 2 loops]; repeat [--] to end. Snake down to the next row.*

» **4** Keep working the rows from * to * until you have filled the required space. Following the instructions for the bottom row (see page 13), attach the DBH to the BS at the bottom.

STITCH NO. 5

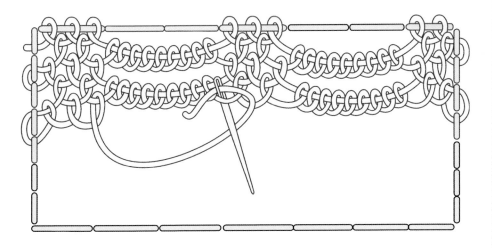

PREPARATION	TOP ROW STITCH LENGTH
BS outline	To accommodate 3 x DBH

» **1** Working LR, [3 x DBH into BS, miss 2 BS]; repeat [--] to end. Go through the nearest BS down the right-hand side that is level with the ridge of the DBH in the row you have just worked. Snake down through the next BS.

» **2** *Working RL, [9 x DBH into large loop, 1 x DBH into small loop, 1 x DBH into small loop]; repeat [--] to end. Snake down to the next row.

» **3** Working LR, [1 x DBH into each small loop i.e. 1 at the end of the group of 9 DBH in the previous row, 1 between the 2 DBH in the middle, and 1 at the beginning of the next group of 9]; repeat [--] to end. Snake down to the next row.*

» **4** Keep working the rows from * to * until you have filled the required space. Following the instructions for the bottom row (see page 13), attach the DBH to the BS at the bottom.

STITCH NO. 6

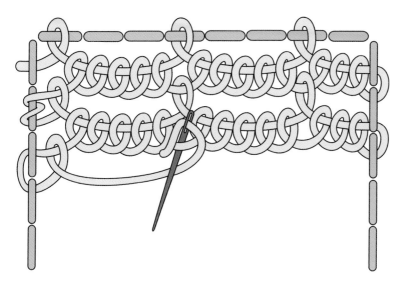

PREPARATION	TOP ROW STITCH LENGTH
BS outline	To accommodate 2 x DBH

» **1** Working LR, [1 x DBH into BS, miss 2 BS]; repeat [--] to end. Go through the nearest BS down the right-hand side that is level with the ridge of the DBH in the row you have just worked. Snake down through the next BS.

» **2** *Working RL, [5 x DBH into large loop, 1 x DBH into small loop]; repeat [--] to end. Snake down to the next row.

» **3** Working LR, 1 x DBH into each small loop. Snake down to the next row.*

» **4** Keep working the rows from * to * until you have filled the required space. Following the instructions for the bottom row (see page 13), attach the DBH to the BS at the bottom.

STITCH NO. 7

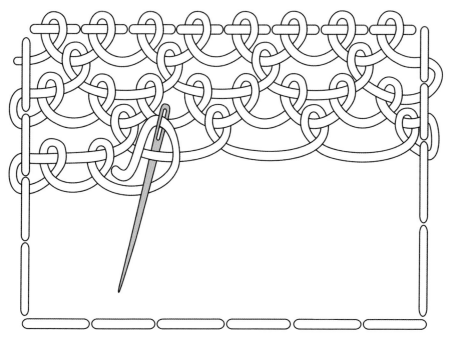

PREPARATION	TOP ROW STITCH LENGTH
BS outline	To accommodate 1 x DBH

» **1** Working LR, 1 x DBH into each BS. Go through the nearest BS down the right-hand side that is level with the ridge of the DBH in the row you have just worked. Snake down through the next BS.

» **2** *Working RL, [miss 1 small loop, 1 x DBH into next small loop]; repeat [--] to end. Snake down to the next row.

» **3** Working LR, 2 x DBH into each large loop. Snake down through the next BS.

» **4** Working LR, [1 x DBH into the small loop between the groups of 2 DBH in the previous row. Miss 1 loop]; repeat [--] to end. Snake down to the next row.*

» **5** Keep working the rows from * to * until you have filled the required space. Following the instructions for the bottom row (see page 13), attach the DBH to the BS at the bottom.

STITCH NO. 8

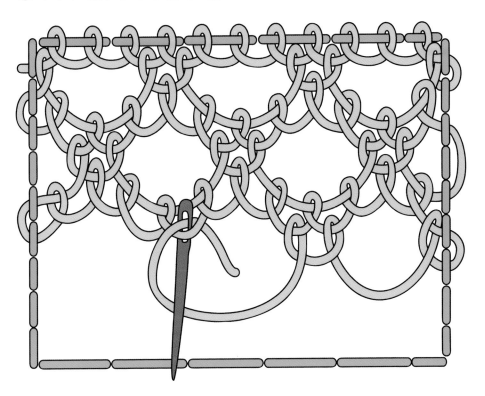

PREPARATION	TOP ROW STITCH LENGTH
BS outline	To accommodate 2 x DBH

» **1** Working LR, 2 x DBH into each BS. Go through the nearest BS down the right-hand side that is level with the ridge of the DBH in the row you have just worked. Snake down through the next BS.

» **2** Working RL, [miss 2 loops, 1 x DBH into next loop, 1 x DBH into next loop]; repeat [--] to end. Snake down to the next row.

» **3** *Working LR, [3 x DBH into large loop, 1 x DBH into small loop]; repeat [--] to end. Snake down to the next row.

» **4** Working RL, [miss 2 loops, 1 x DBH into next loop, 1 x DBH into next loop]. Make sure that you go into the two loops in the middle of the group of three in the previous row. Repeat [--] to end. Snake down to the next row.*

» **5** Keep working the rows from * to * until you have filled the required space. Following the instructions for the bottom row (see page 13), attach the DBH to the BS at the bottom.

STITCH NO. 9

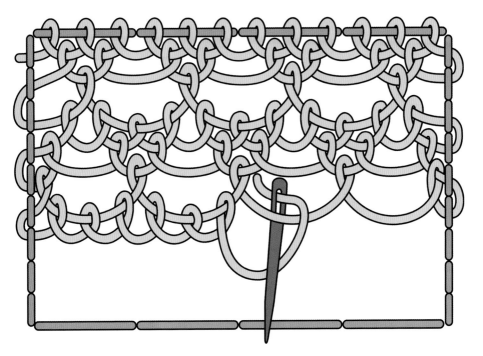

PREPARATION	TOP ROW STITCH LENGTH
BS outline	To accommodate 3 x DBH

» **1** Working LR, 3 x DBH into each BS. Go through the nearest BS down the right-hand side that is level with the ridge of the DBH in the row you have just worked. Snake down through the next BS.

» **2** *Working RL, [1 x DBH into next loop, 1 x DBH into next loop, miss 1 loop]; repeat [--] to end. Snake down to the next row.

» **3** Working LR, [1 x DBH in small loop, miss large loop]; repeat [--] to end. Snake down to the next row.

» **4** Working LR, 3 x DBH into each large loop. Snake down to the next row.*

» **5** Keep working the rows from * to * until you have filled the required space. Following the instructions for the bottom row (see page 13), attach the DBH to the BS at the bottom.

STITCH NO. 10

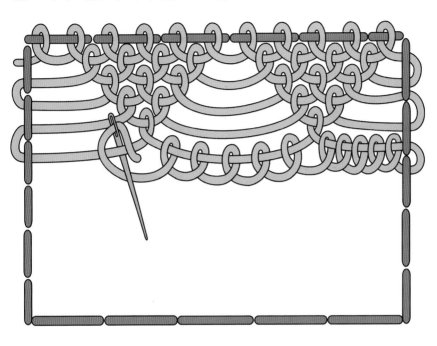

PREPARATION	TOP ROW STITCH LENGTH
BS outline	To accommodate 2 x DBH

» **1** Working LR, 2 x DBH into each BS. Go through the nearest BS down the right-hand side that is level with the ridge of the DBH in the row you have just worked. Snake down through the next BS.

» **2** *Working RL, [miss 1 loop, 1 x DBH into each of the next 4 loops]; repeat [--] to end. Snake down to the next row.

» **3** Working LR, [miss large loop, 1 x DBH into each of the next 3 loops]; repeat [--] to end. Snake down to the next row.

» **4** Working RL, [miss large loop, 1 x DBH into each of the next 2 loops]; repeat [--] to end. Snake down to the next row.

» **5** Working LR, [miss large loop, 1 x DBH into the small loop]; repeat [--] to end. Snake down to the next row.

» **6** Working RL, 5 x DBH into each large loop. Snake down to the next row.*

» **7** Keep working the rows from * to * until you have filled the required space. Following the instructions for the bottom row (see page 13), attach the DBH to the BS at the bottom.

STITCH NO. 11

PREPARATION	TOP ROW STITCH LENGTH
BS outline	To accommodate 2 x DBH

» **1** Working LR, 1 x DBH into each BS. Go through the nearest BS down the right-hand side that is level with the ridge of the DBH in the row you have just worked. Snake down through the next BS.

» **2** *Working RL, [1 x DBH into large loop, 1 x DBH into large loop, 1 x DBH into large loop, 3 x DBH into large loop]; repeat [--] to end. Snake down to the next row.

» **3** Working LR, [1 x DBH into large loop, 1 x DBH into large loop, 1 x DBH into large loop, 3 x DBH into large loop]; repeat [--] to end. Snake down to the next row.

» **4** Working RL, [3 x DBH into large loop, 1 x DBH into large loop, 1 x DBH into large loop, 1 x DBH into large loop]; repeat [--] to end. Snake down to the next row.

» **5** Working LR, [1 x DBH into large loop, 1 x DBH into large loop, 3 x DBH into large loop, 1 x DBH into large loop]; repeat [--] to end. Snake down to the next row.*

» **6** Keep working the rows from * to * until you have filled the required space. Following the instructions for the bottom row (see page 13), attach the DBH to the BS at the bottom.

STITCH NO. 13

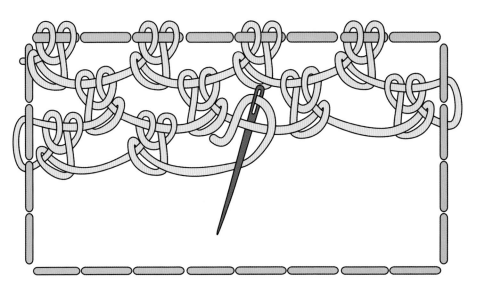

PREPARATION	TOP ROW STITCH LENGTH
BS outline	To accommodate 2 x DBH

» **1** Working LR, [2 x DBH into BS, needle over and then under the loop that leads up to the group, work a 2G+1 (see box below), miss 1 x BS]; repeat [--] to end. Go through the nearest BS down the right-hand side that is level with the ridge of the DBH in the row you have just worked. Snake down through the next BS.

» **2** *Working RL, work a 2G+1 into each large loop. Snake down to the next row.

» **3** Working LR, work a 2G+1 into each large loop. Snake down to the next row.*

» **4** Keep working the rows from * to * until you have filled the required space. Following the instructions for the bottom row (see page 13), attach the DBH to the BS at the bottom.

2G+1

Making sure that the working thread is lying under the needle, pull through to form a buttonhole stitch that lies horizontally below the group of two DBH. This is called a Two Group Plus One (2G+1).

STITCH NO. 14

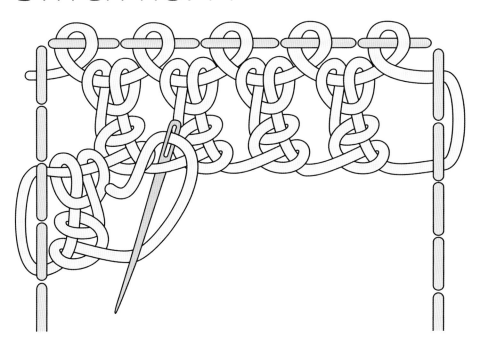

PREPARATION	TOP ROW STITCH LENGTH
BS outline	To accommodate 2 x DBH

» **1** Working LR, 1 x DBH into each BS. Go through the nearest BS down the right-hand side that is level with the ridge of the DBH in the row you have just worked. Snake down through the next BS.

» **2** ^Working RL, [2 x DBH into large loop, noodle over and then under the loop that leads up to the group, work a 2G+2 (see box)]; repeat [--] into every large loop.

» **3** Working LR, work a 2G+2 into each large loop. Snake down to the next row.*

» **4** Keep working the rows from * to * until you have filled the required space. Following the instructions for the bottom row (see page 13), attach the DBH to the BS at the bottom, leaving out the additional horizontal buttonhole stitch.

2G+2

Making sure that the working thread is lying under the needle, pull through to form a buttonhole stitch that lies horizontally below the group of two DBH. Work a second horizontal buttonhole stitch below that. This is called a Two Group Plus Two (2G+2).

STITCH NO. 15

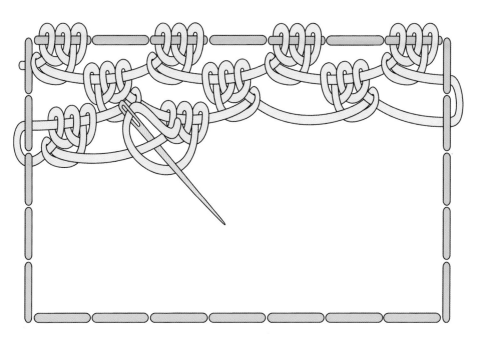

PREPARATION	TOP ROW STITCH LENGTH
BS outline	To accommodate 3 x DBH

» **1** Working LR, [3 x DBH into BS, needle over and then under the loop that leads up to the group, work a 3G+1 (see box), miss 1 x BS]; repeat [--] to end. Go through the nearest BS down the right-hand side that is level with the ridge of the DBH in the row you have just worked. Snake down through the next BS.

» **2** *Working RL, work a 3G+1 into each large loop. Snake down to the next row.

» **3** Working LR, work a 3G+1 into each large loop. Snake down to the next row.*

» **4** Keep working the rows from * to * until you have filled the required space. Following the instructions for the bottom row (see page 13), attach the DBH to the BS at the bottom, leaving out the additional horizontal buttonhole.

3G+1

Making sure that the working thread is lying under the needle, pull through to form a buttonhole stitch that lies horizontally below the group of three DBH. This is called a Three Group Plus One (3G+1).

STITCH NO. 16

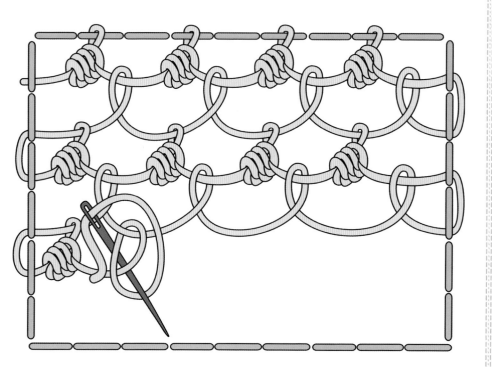

PREPARATION	TOP ROW STITCH LENGTH
BS outline	To accommodate 1 x DBH

» **1** Working LR, work a 4GOy (see box) and repeat to end. Go through the nearest BS down the right-hand side that is level with the ridge of the DBH in the row you have just worked. Snake down through the next BS.

» **2** *Working RL, 1 x DBH into each loop between the Oyster groups. Snake down to the next row.

» **3** Working LR, 1 x 4GOy into each loop. Snake down to the next row.*

» **4** Keep working the rows from * to * until you have filled the required space. Following the instructions for the bottom row (see page 13), attach the DBH to the BS at the bottom.

4GOy

This terms means 'Four Group Oyster', and is made with the following instructions: miss 1 x BS, 1 x DBH, pull (but not too tightly) and then work 4 x DBH onto the loop leading to the main DBH, starting from the bottom and working up to the top.

STITCH NO. 17

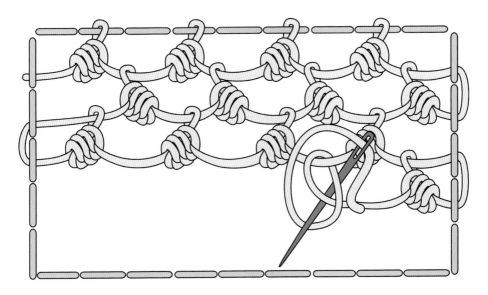

PREPARATION	TOP ROW STITCH LENGTH
BS outline	To accommodate 1 x DBH

» **1** Working LR, work a 4GOy (see box on page 47) and repeat to end. Go through the nearest BS down the right-hand side that is level with the ridge of the DBH in the row you have just worked. Snake down through the next BS.

» **2** *Working RL, 1 x 4GOy into each loop. Snake down to the next row.

» **3** Working LR, 1 x 4GOy into each loop. Snake down to the next row.*

» **4** Keep working the rows from * to * until you have filled the required space. Following the instructions for the bottom row (see page 13), attach the DBH to the BS at the bottom.

STITCH NO. 22

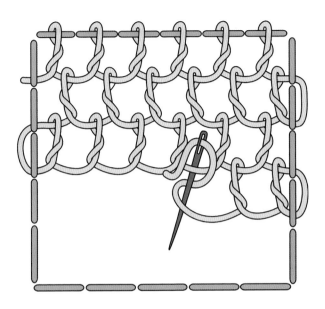

PREPARATION	TOP ROW STITCH LENGTH
BS outline	To accommodate 1 x DBH

» **1** Working LR, 1 x TB (see below) into each BS. Go through the nearest BS down the right-hand side that is level with the ridge of the TB in the row you have just worked. Snake down through the next BS.

» **2** *Working RL, work 1 x TB into each loop. Snake down to the next row.

» **3** Working LR, 1 x TB into each loop. Snake down to the next row.*

» **4** Keep working the rows from * to * until you have filled the required space. Following the instructions for the bottom row (see page 13), attach the tulle bars to the BS at the bottom.

To work a tulle bar

Take your needle over and under the BS or the loop in the row above, as you would for a DBH. Take the thread under and over the needle to create an additional twist, thereby creating what is referred to in these instructions as a tulle bar (TB).

STITCH NO. 23

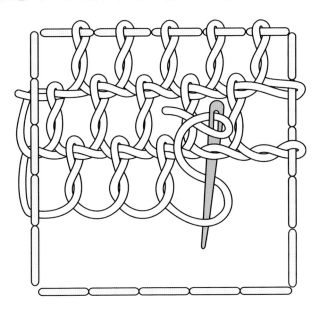

PREPARATION	TOP ROW STITCH LENGTH
BS outline	To accommodate 1 x DBH

» **1** Working LR, 1 x TB (see box on page 51) into each BS. Go through the nearest BS down the right-hand side that is level with the ridge of the TB in the row you have just worked. Working RL, whip once into each loop. Go through the nearest BS down the left-hand side that is level with the ridge of the TB and whipping. Snake down through the next BS.

» **2** *Working LR, work 1 x TB into each loop. Go through the nearest BS down the right-hand side that is level with the ridge of the TB in the row you have just worked. Working RL, whip once into each loop. Go through the nearest BS down the left-hand side that is level with the ridge of the TB and whipping. Snake down to the next row.*

» **3** Keep working the row from * to * until you have filled the required space. Following the instructions for the bottom row (see page 13), attach the tulle bars to the BS at the bottom.

STITCH NO. 24

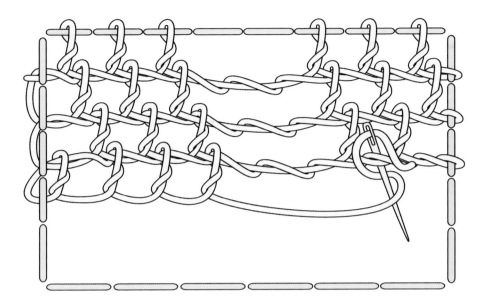

PREPARATION	TOP ROW STITCH LENGTH
BS outline	To accommodate 1 x DBH

» **1** Working LR, [1 x TB (see box on page 51), 1 x TB, 1 x TB, miss 2 x BS]; repeat [--] to end. Go through the nearest BS down the right-hand side that is level with the ridge of the TB in the row you have just worked. Working RL, whip once into each small loop and twice into each large loop. Go through the nearest BS down the left-hand side that is level with the ridge of the TB and whipping. Snake down through the next BS.

» **2** *Working LR, work 1 x TB into each small loop and 1 x TB into the start of the large loop, pulling it towards the left so that it groups with those in the small loops. Go through the nearest BS down the right-hand side that is level with the ridge of the TB in the row you have just worked. Working RL, whip once into each loop. Go through the nearest BS down the left-hand side that is level with the ridge of the TB and whipping. Snake down to the next row.

» **3** Work another row in the same way.

» **4** Working LR, 1 x TB, then: work 1 x TB into each small loop, 1 x TB into the start of the large loop, pulling it towards the left so that it groups with those in the small loops. Go through the nearest BS down the right-hand side that is level with the ridge of the TB in the row you have just worked. Working RL, whip once into each loop. Go through the nearest BS down the left-hand side that is level with the ridge of the TB and whipping. Snake down to the next row.*

» **5** Keep working the rows from * to * until you have filled the required space. Following the instructions for the bottom row (see page 13), attach the tulle bars to the BS at the bottom.

STITCH NO. 25

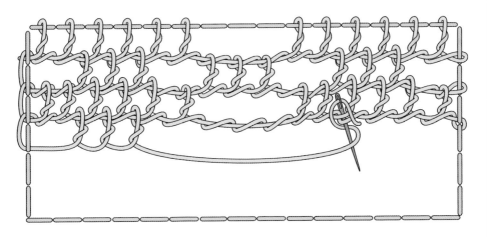

PREPARATION	TOP ROW STITCH LENGTH
BS outline	To accommodate 1 x DBH

» **1** Working LR, [1 x TB (see box on page 51), 1 x TB, 1 x TB, 1 x TB, 1 x TB, 1 x TB, miss 3 x BS]; repeat [--] to end. Go through the nearest BS down the right-hand side that is level with the ridge of the TB in the row you have just worked. Working RL, whip once into each small loop and four times into each large loop. Go through the nearest BS down the left-hand side that is level with the ridge of the TB and whipping. Snake down through the next BS.

» **2** *Working LR, [miss 1 small loop, 1 x TB, 1 x TB, 1 x TB, miss 1 small loop, 3 x TB into large loop]; repeat [--] to end. Go through the nearest BS down the right-hand side that is level with the ridge of the TB in the row you have just worked. Working RL, whip once into each small loop and four times into each large loop. Go through the nearest BS down the left-hand side that is level with the ridge of the TB and whipping. Snake down through the next BS.

» **3** Working LR, [2 x TB into large loop, 1 x TB into each of the next small loops, 2 x TB into large loop, miss 2 small loops]; repeat [--] to end. Go through the nearest BS down the right-hand side that is level with the ridge of the TB in the row you have just worked. Working RL, whip once into each small loop and four times into each large loop. Go through the nearest BS down the left-hand side that is level with the ridge of the TB and whipping. Snake down through the next BS.*

» **4** Keep working the rows from * to * until you have filled the required space. Following the instructions for the bottom row (see page 13), attach the tulle bars to the BS at the bottom.

STITCH NO. 26

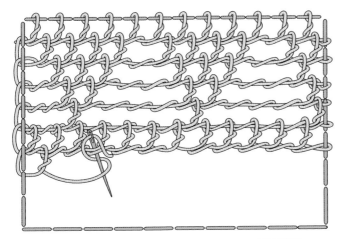

PREPARATION	TOP ROW STITCH LENGTH
BS outline	To accommodate 1 x DBH

» **1** Working LR, 1 x TB (see box on page 51) into each BS. Go through the nearest BS down the right-hand side that is level with the ridge of the TB in the row you have just worked. Working RL, whip once into each small loop and four times into each large loop. Go through the nearest BS down the left-hand side that is level with the ridge of the TB and whipping. Snake down through the next BS.

» **2** *Working LR, [1 x TB, 1 x TB, 1 x TB, 1 x TB, miss 1 loop]; repeat [--] to end. Return to the left side as you did in the previous row, whipping once into each small loop and twice into each large loop. Go through the nearest BS down the left-hand side that is level with the ridge of the TB and whipping. Snake down through the next BS.

» **3** Working LR, 1 x TB (3 x TB) into each small loop. Return to the left side as you did in the previous row, whipping once into each small loop and three times into each large loop. Go through the nearest BS down the left-hand side that is level with the ridge of the TB and whipping. Snake down through the next BS.

» **4** Working LR, 1 x TB (2 x TB) into each small loop. Return to the left side as you did in the previous row, whipping once into each small loop and four times into each large loop. Go through the nearest BS down the left-hand side that is level with the ridge of the TB and whipping. Snake down through the next BS.

» **5** Working LR, 1 x TB into the small loop. Return to the left side as you did in the previous row, whipping once into each small loop and five times into each large loop. Go through the nearest BS down the left-hand side that is level with the ridge of the TB and whipping. Snake down through the next BS.

» **6** Working LR, 5 x TB into each large loop. Return to the left side as you did in the previous row, whipping once into each small loop. Go through the nearest BS down the left-hand side that is level with the ridge of the TB and whipping. Snake down through the next BS.*

» **7** Keep working the rows from * to * until you have filled the required space. Following the instructions for the bottom row (see page 13), attach the tulle bars to the BS at the bottom.

STITCH NO. 27

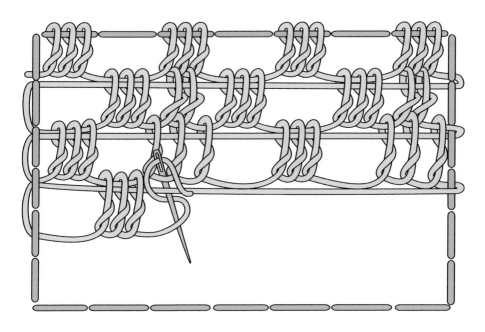

PREPARATION	TOP ROW STITCH LENGTH
BS outline	To accommodate 3 x DBH

» **1** Working LR, [3 x TB (see box on page 51) into BS, miss 1 x BS]; repeat [--] to end. Go through the nearest BS down the right-hand side that is level with the ridge of the TB in the row you have just worked. Take the thread back to the left and go under the BS that is level with where you went in on the right-hand side (usually, but not always, under the same BS where you started). This forms the 'cord'. Snake down through the next BS.

» **2** *Working LR, [miss the first group and incorporate cord as you work, 3 x TB into the large loop, 1 x TB into small loop, 1 x TB into small loop, 3 x TB into large loop]; repeat [--] to end. Form the cord as you did in the previous row and snake down through the next BS.

» **3** Working LR, [3 x TB into large loop, 1 x TB into the loop after the next group, 1 x TB between the 2 x TB in the previous row, 1 x TB into loop before next group]; repeat [--] to end. Form the cord as you did in the previous row and snake down through the next BS.*

» **4** Keep working the rows from * to * until you have filled the required space. Following the instructions for the bottom row (see page 13), attach the tulle bars to the BS at the bottom.

STITCH NO. 33

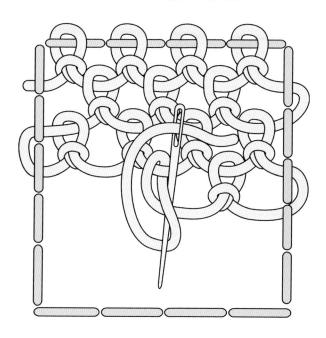

PREPARATION	TOP ROW STITCH LENGTH
BS outline	To accommodate 1 x DBH

» **1** Working LR, [1 x DBH, take the needle back under the loop before the DBH, twist thread over and under the needle, pull through to form small knot]; repeat [--] into each BS. Go through the nearest DC down the right-hand side that is level with the ridge of the DBH in the row you have just worked. Snake down through the next BS.

» **2** *Working RL, [1 x DBH, take needle back under the loop before the DBH, twist thread over and under the needle, pull through to form small knot]; repeat [--] into each loop. Go through the nearest BS down the right-hand side that is level with the ridge of the DBH in the row you have just worked. Snake down through the next BS.

» **3** Working LR, [1 x DBH, take needle back under the loop before the DBH, twist thread over and under the needle, pull through to form small knot]; repeat [--] into each loop. Go through the nearest BS down the right-hand side that is level with the ridge of the DBH in the row you have just worked. Snake down through the next BS.*

» **4** Keep working the rows from * to * until you have filled the required space. Following the instructions for the bottom row (see page 13), attach the tulle bars to the BS at the bottom.

STITCH NO. 34

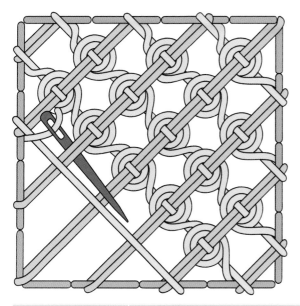

PREPARATION	TOP ROW STITCH LENGTH
BS outline	To accommodate 2 x DBH

First layer

» Working diagonally over the space, stitch the first layer (darker lines). Come up from outside, close to the BS line. Lay the thread at a 45° angle across the whole area. Go over and under the nearest BS. Take the thread back to where you started, going under the BS line and into the fabric. Taking into account that the spacing of the stitches should allow space for the circles in the second layer, cover the entire shape with long diagonal double stitches.

Second layer

» **1** The second layer (paler lines) is worked at right angles to the first layer. Come up from the outside, close to the BS line, and lay the thread at a 45° angle across the whole area. Go over and under the nearest BS. This forms the middle line.

» **2** Working in a circle, cross over the middle line, go under the side stitch (formed by the first

layer of stitching), go over the middle line, go under the side stitch on the other side, go over the middle line at the top and go under the side stitch on the first side. This forms one circle.

» **3** Work a second concentric circle: go over the middle line, go under the side stitch on the other side, go over the middle line at the top and go under the side stitch on the first side. This forms the second circle. Then, go over the middle line and under the next side stitch formed by the first layer.

» **4** Form the next two concentric circles by working in the opposite direction to the first two.

» **5** Keep working down the line in this way until you reach the bottom. Take your thread over the middle line, go under the BS line and then into the fabric. Taking into account the spacing of the stitches, complete the second layer of stitching.

BEADED STITCHES

STITCH NO. 1†

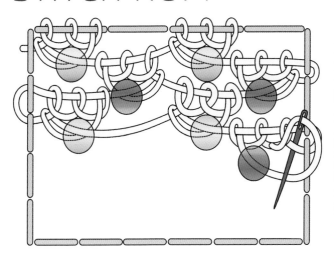

3G+1B

Making sure that the working thread is lying under the needle, pull through to form a buttonhole stitch that lies horizontally below the group of two DBH with the thread lying behind the bead. This is called a Three Group Plus One Beaded (3G+1B).

PREPARATION	TOP ROW STITCH LENGTH
BS outline	To accommodate 3 x DBH

» **1** Working LR, [3 x DBH into BS, pick up a bead and slide it to the bottom of the thread where it comes out of the DBH, needle over and then under the loop that leads up to the group, work a 3G+1B (see box), miss 1 x BS]; repeat [--] to end. Go through the nearest BS down the right-hand side that is level with the ridge of the DBH in the row you have just worked. Snake down through the next BS.

» **2** *Working RL, work a 3G+1B into each large loop. Snake down to the next row.

» **3** Working LR, work a 3G+1B into each large loop. Snake down to the next row.*

» **4** Keep working rows * to * in this way until you have filled the required space. Following the instructions for the bottom row (see page 13), attach the DBH to the BS at the bottom, leaving out the additional horizontal buttonhole and bead.

† Based on Numbered Stitch No. 15, see page 45.

STITCH NO. 2[†]

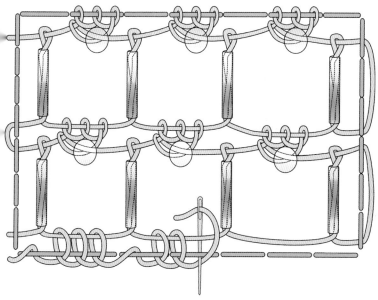

PREPARATION	TOP ROW STITCH LENGTH
BS outline	To accommodate 3 x DBH

» **1** Working LR, [3 x DBH into BS, pick up a bead and slide it to the bottom of the thread where it comes out of the DBH, needle over and then under the loop that leads up to the group, work a 3G+1B (see box on page 67), miss 1 x BS]; repeat [--] to end. Go through the nearest BS down the right hand side that is level with the ridge of the DBH in the row you have just worked. Snake down through the next BS, taking note of the wider spacing that you will need to accommodate the bugle bead.

» **2** *Working RL, [pick up a bugle bead, work a DBH by going over and under the loop at the top, taking the thread back down the bead and going over the thread leading up to the bead to create the buttonhole formation]; repeat [--] to end. Snake down to the next row.

» **3** Working LR, work a 3G+1B into each loop. Snake down to the next row, taking note of the wider spacing that you will need to accommodate the bugle bead.*

» **4** Keep working rows * to * in this way until you have filled the required space. Try to end on a row that incorporates the bugle beads, so that you can finish off with groups of 3 at the bottom edge. Following the instructions for the bottom row (see page 13), attach the DBS to the BS at the bottom, leaving out the additional horizontal buttonhole and bead.

---

† Based on Numbered Stitch No. 15, see page 45.

STITCH NO. 3[†]

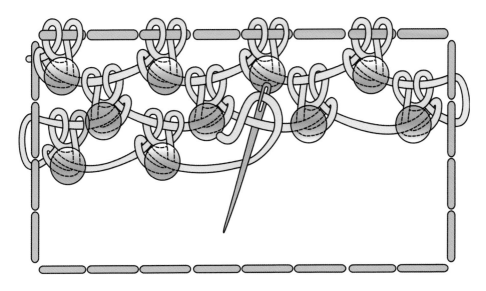

PREPARATION	TOP ROW STITCH LENGTH
BS outline	To accommodate 2 x DBH

» **1** Working LR, [2 x DBH into BS, pick up a bead and slide it to the bottom of the thread where it comes out of the DBH, needle over and then under the loop that leads up to the group, work a 2G+1B (see box), miss 1 x BS]; repeat [--] to end. Go through the nearest BS down the right-hand side that is level with the ridge of the DBH in the row you have just worked. Snake down through the next BS.

» **2** Working RL, work a 2G+1B into each large loop. Snake down to the next row.

» **3** Working LR, work a 2G+1B into each large loop. Snake down to the next row.*

» **4** Keep working rows * to * in this way until you have filled the required space. Following the instructions for the bottom row (see page 13), attach the DBH to the BS at the bottom, leaving out the additional horizontal buttonhole and bead.

2G+1B

Making sure that the working thread is lying under the needle, pull through to form a buttonhole stitch that lies horizontally below the group of two DBH with the thread lying behind the bead. This is called a Two Group Plus One Beaded (2G+1B).

STITCH NO. 4[†]

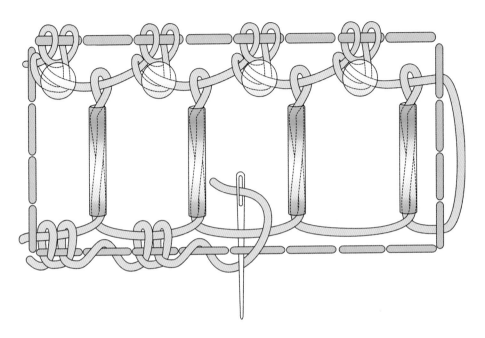

PREPARATION	TOP ROW STITCH LENGTH
BS outline	To accommodate 2 x DBH

» **1** Working LR, [2 x DBH into BS, pick up a bead and slide it to the bottom of the thread where it comes out of the DBH, needle over and then under the loop that leads up to the group, work a 2G+1B (see box on page 71), miss 1 x BS]; repeat [--] to end. Go through the nearest BS down the right-hand side that is level with the ridge of the DBH in the row you have just worked. Snake down through the next BS, taking note of the wider spacing that you will need to accommodate the bugle bead.

» **2** *Working RL, [pick up a bugle bead, work a DBH by going over and under the loop at the top, taking the thread back down the bead and going over the thread leading up to the bead to create the buttonhole formation]; repeat [--] to end. Snake down to the next row.

» **3** Working LR, work a 2G+1B into each loop. Snake down to the next row, taking note of the wider spacing that you will need to accommodate the bugle bead.*

» **4** Keep working rows * to * in this way until you have filled the required space. Try to end on a row that incorporates the bugle beads, so that you can finish off with groups of 2 at the bottom edge. Following the instructions for the bottom row (see page 13), attach the DBH to the BS at the bottom, leaving out the additional horizontal buttonhole and bead.

STITCH NO. 1†

PREPARATION	TOP ROW STITCH LENGTH
BS outline	To accommodate 2 x DBH

2G+3

Making sure that the working thread is lying under the needle, pull through to form a buttonhole stitch that lies horizontally below the group of two DBH. Work two more DBH in the same way. This is called a Two Group Plus Three (2G+3).

Please turn to page 77 to view stitch diagram.

» **1** Working LR, 2 x DBH into each BS. Go into the fabric at the end of the row and come up again to start the next row, where the ridge of DBH in that row will lie.

» **2** Working RL, [miss 2 loops, 1 x DBH into next loop, 1 x DBH into next loop]; repeat [--] to end. Go into the fabric at the end of the row and come up again to start the next row, where the ridge of DBH in that row will lie

» **3** Working LR, [3 x DBH into large loop, 1 x DBH into small loop]; repeat [--] to end. Go into the fabric at the end of the row and come up again to start the next row, where the ridge of DBH in that row will lie.

» **4** Working RL, miss 2 loops, [1 x DBH into next loop, 1 x DBH into next loop]; repeat [--] to end. Make sure that you go into the two loops in the middle of the group of three in the previous row. Go into the fabric at the end of the row and come up again to start the next row, where the ridge of DBH in that row will lie.

» **5** Working LR, [miss large loop, 1 DBH into small loop]; repeat [--] to end. Go into the fabric, turn your work over and catch a bit of the fabric. Come up to the top in the same place. Working RL, whip once into each small loop and twice into each large loop. Go into the fabric at the end of the row and come up again to start the next row, where the base of the gap formed in that row will lie.

» **6** Working LR, [2 x DBH into large loop, needle over and then under the loop that leads up to the group, work a 2G+3 (see box on previous page), move to next large loop]; repeat [--] to end. Go into the fabric at the end of the row and come up again to start the next row, where the ridge of DBH in that row will lie.

» **7** Working RL, work 2 x DBH into each large loop. Go into the fabric at the end of the row and come up again to start the next row, where the ridge of DBH in that row will lie.

---

† Insertion lace.

» **8** Working LR, work 1 x DBH into each small loop. Go into the fabric at the end of the row and come up again to start the next row, where the ridge of DBH in that row will lie.

» **9** Working RL, [2 x DBH, 1 x DBH with picot, 2 x DBH into large loop]; repeat [--] to end and finish off the thread.

» **10** Thread 2mm (⅟₁₆in) silk ribbon onto a size 22 or larger tapestry (blunt-end) needle. Bring the needle up in the middle of the gap created by Row 6. Weave the ribbon over and under the bars. Take the needle to the back of the fabric and end off the ribbon.

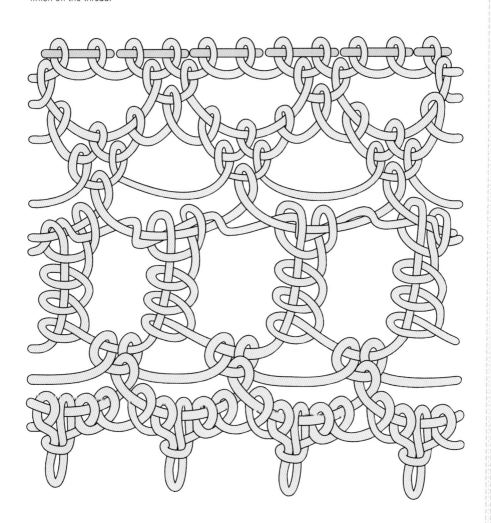

STITCH NO. 2[†]

PREPARATION	TOP ROW STITCH LENGTH
BS line along top edge	To accommodate 2 x DBH

» **1** Working LR, 2 x DBH into each BS. Go into the fabric at the end of the row and come up again to start the next row where the ridge of DBH in that row will lie.

» **2** Working RL, [miss 2 loops, 1 x DBH into next loop, 1 x DBH into next loop]; repeat [--] to end. Go into the fabric at the end of the row and come up again to start the next row, where the ridge of DBH in that row will lie.

» **3** Working LR, [3 x DBH into large loop, 1 x DBH into small loop]; repeat [--] to end. Go into the fabric at the end of the row and come up again to start the next row, where the ridge of DBH in that row will lie.

» **4** Working RL, [miss 2 loops, 1 x DBH into next loop, 1 x DBH into next loop]; repeat [--] to end. Make sure that you go into the two loops in the middle of the group of three in the previous row. Go into the fabric at the end of the row and come up again to start the next row, where the ridge of DBH in that row will lie.

» **5** Working LR, [miss large loop, 1 DBH into small loop]; repeat [--] to end. Go into the fabric, turn your work over and catch a bit of the fabric. Come up to the top in the same place. Working RL, whip once into each small loop and twice into each large loop. Go into the fabric at the end of the row and come up again to start the next row, where the base of the gap formed in that row will lie.

» **6** Working LR, [2 x DBH into large loop, needle over and then under the loop that leads up to the group, work a 2G+3 (see box on page 75), move to next large loop]; repeat [--] to end.

» **7** Go into the fabric, turn your work over and catch a bit of the fabric. Come up to the top in the same place. Working RL, whip once into each small loop and twice into each large loop. Go into the fabric at the end of the row and come up again to start the next row, where the base of the gap formed in that row will lie.

» **8** Working LR, [2 x DBH into large loop, needle over and then under the loop that leads up to the group, work a 2G+3, move to next large loop]; repeat [--] to end. Go into the fabric at the end of the row and come up again to start the next row, where the ridge of DBH in that row will lie.

» **9** Working RL, [2 x DBH, 1 x DBH with picot, 2 x DBH into large loop]; repeat [--] to end and finish off the thread.

» **10** Thread 2mm (1/16in) silk ribbon onto a size 22 or larger tapestry (blunt-end) needle. Bring the needle up in the middle of the gap created by Row 6. Weave the ribbon over and under the bars. Take the needle to the back of the fabric. Come up in the middle of the gap created by Row 8. Weave the ribbon over and under the bars. Take the needle to the back of the fabric and end off the ribbon.

Please turn to page 81 to view stitch diagram.

[†] *Insertion lace.*

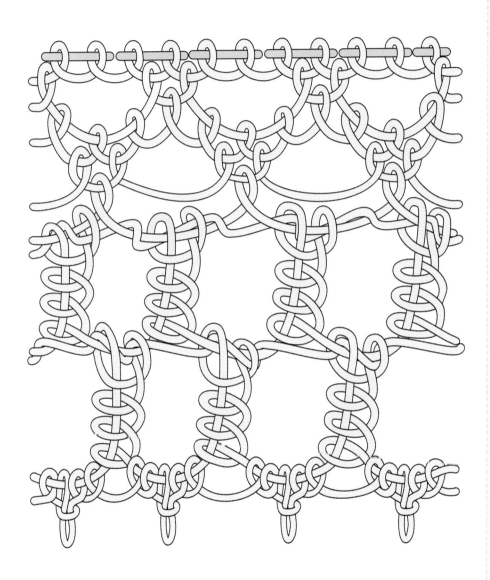

STITCH NO. 3[†]

PREPARATION	TOP ROW STITCH LENGTH
BS line along top edge	To accommodate 2 x DBH

» **1** Working LR, 2 x DBH into each BS. Go into the fabric at the end of the row and come up again to start the next row, where the ridge of DBH in that row will lie.

» **2** Working RL, [miss 2 loops, 1 x DBH into next loop, 1 x DBH into next loop]; repeat [--] to end. Go into the fabric at the end of the row and come up again to start the next row, where the ridge of DBH in that row will lie.

» **3** Working LR, [3 x DBH into large loop, 1 x DBH into small loop]; repeat [--] to end. Go into the fabric at the end of the row and come up again to start the next row, where the ridge of DBH in that row will lie.

» **4** Working RL, [miss 2 loops, 1 x DBH into next loop, 1 x DBH into next loop]; repeat [--] to end. Make sure that you go into the two loops in the middle of the group of three in the previous row. Go into the fabric at the end of the row and come up again to start the next row where the ridge of DBH in that row will lie.

» **5** Working LR, [miss large loop, 1 DBH into small loop]; repeat [--] to end. Go into the fabric, turn your work over and catch a bit of the fabric. Come up to the top in the same place. Working RL, whip once into each small loop and twice into each large loop. Go into the fabric at the end of the row and come up again to start the next row, where the base of the gap formed in that row will lie.

» **6** Working LR, [2 x DBH into large loop, needle over and then under the loop that leads up to the group, work a 2G+3 (see box on page 75), move to next large loop]; repeat [--] to end.

» **7** Go into the fabric, turn your work over and catch a bit of the fabric. Come up to the top in the same place. Working RL, whip once into each small loop and twice into each large loop. Go into the fabric at the end of the row and come up again to start the next row, where the base of the gap formed in that row will lie.

» **8** Working LR, [2 x DBH into large loop, needle over and then under the loop that led up to the group, work a 2G+3, move to next large loop]; repeat [--] to end. Go into the fabric at the end of the row and come up again to start the next row, where the ridge of DBH in that row will lie.

» **9** Working RL, [2 x DBH into each available loop]; repeat [--] to end.

» **10** Working RL, [1 x DBH, 1 x DBH with picot, 1 x DBH into large loop]; repeat [--] to end and finish off the thread.

» **11** Thread 2mm (1⁄16in) silk ribbon onto a size 22 or larger tapestry (blunt-end) needle. Bring the needle up in the middle of the gap created by Row 6. Weave the ribbon over and under the bars. Take the needle to the back of the fabric. Come up in the middle of the gap created by Row 8. Weave the ribbon over and under the bars. Take the needle to the back of the fabric and end off the ribbon.

> **Please turn to page 85 to view stitch diagram.**

STITCH NO. 4[†]

PREPARATION	TOP ROW STITCH LENGTH
BS line along top, left and right edge	To accommodate 3 x DBH

3G+bead

Making sure that the working thread is lying under the needle, pull through to form a buttonhole stitch that lies horizontally below the group of three DBS. Make sure that the working thread lies behind the bead. This is called a 3G+bead.

» **1** Working LR, 3 x DBH into the first BS. Pick up a bead, pulling it down the thread to touch the third DBH. Take the needle over and then under the loop that leads up to the group. Work a 3G+bead (see box). Miss the next BS. Work a 3G+bead into the next BS and into every alternate BS until you reach the end. Go into the fabric at the end of the row and come up again to start the next row, where the ridge of DBH in that row will lie.

» **2** Working RL, work a 3G+bead into each large loop in the previous row. Go into the fabric at the end of the row and come up again to start the next row, where the ridge of DBH in that row will lie.

» **3** Working LR, work a 3G+bead into each large loop in the previous row. Go into the fabric at the end of the row and come up again to start the next row, where the ridge of DBH in that row will lie.

» **4** Working RL, 2 x DBH into each large loop. Go into the fabric at the end of the row and come up again to start the next row, where the ridge of DBH in that row will lie.

» **5** Working LR, 1 x DBH into the small loop between the 2 x DBH in the previous row. Go into the fabric, turn your work over and catch a bit of the fabric. Come up to the top in the same place. Working RL, whip once into each small loop and twice into each large loop. Go into the fabric at the end of the row and come up again to start the next row, where the base of the gap formed in that row will lie.

» **6** Working LR, [2 x DBH into large loop, needle over and then under the loop that leads up to the group, work a 2G+3 (see box on page 75), move to next large loop]; repeat [--] to end.

Please turn to page 89 to view stitch diagram.

[†] *Insertion lace.*

» **7** Go into the fabric, turn your work over and catch a bit of the fabric. Come up to the top in the same place. Working RL, whip once into each small loop and twice into each large loop. Go into the fabric at the end of the row and come up again to start the next row, where the base of the gap formed in that row will lie.

» **8** Working LR, [2 x DBH into large loop, needle over and then under the loop that leads up to the group, work a 2G+3, move to next large loop]; repeat [--] to end. Go into the fabric at the end of the row and come up again to start the next row, where the ridge of DBH in that row will lie.

» **9** Working RL, [2 x DBH, 1 x DBH with picot, 2 x DBH into large loop]; repeat [--] to end and finish off the thread.

» **10** Thread 2mm (1⁄16in) silk ribbon onto a size 22 or larger tapestry (blunt-end) needle. Bring the needle up in the middle of the gap created by Row 6. Weave the ribbon over and under the bars. Take the needle to the back of the fabric. Come up in the middle of the gap created by Row 8. Weave the ribbon over and under the bars. Take the needle to the back of the fabric and end off the ribbon.

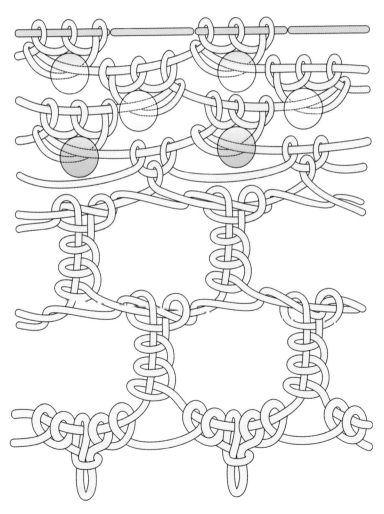

STITCH NO. 5[†]

PREPARATION	TOP ROW STITCH LENGTH
BS line along top, left and right edge	To accommodate 2 x DBH

» **1** Working LR, 2 x DBH into each BS. Go into the fabric at the end of the row and come up again to start the next row, where the ridge of DBH in that row will lie.

» **2** Working RL, [miss 2 loops, 1 x DBH into next loop, 1 x DBH into next loop]; repeat [--] to end. Go into the fabric at the end of the row and come up again to start the next row, where the ridge of DBH in that row will lie.

» **3** Working LR, [3 x DBH into large loop, 1 x DBH into small loop]; repeat [--] to end. Go into the fabric at the end of the row and come up again to start the next row, where the ridge of DBH in that row will lie.

» **4** Working RL, [miss 2 loops, 1 x DBH into next loop, 1 x DBH into next loop]; repeat [--] to end. Make sure that you go into the two loops in the middle of the group of three in the previous row.

» **5** Working LR, [3 x DBH into large loop, 1 x DBH into small loop]; repeat [--] to end. Go into the fabric at the end of the row and come up again to start the next row, where the ridge of DBH in that row will lie.

» **6** Working RL, [miss 2 loops, 1 x DBH into next loop, 1 x DBH into next loop]; repeat [--] to end. Make sure that you go into the two loops in the middle of the group of three in the previous row.

Go into the fabric, turn your work over and catch a bit of the fabric. Come up to the top in the same place. Working LR, whip twice into each large loop. Go into the fabric at the end of the row and end off.

» **7** Work a TB (see box on page 51) into each loop in the row. When you reach the other side, go into the fabric, turn your work over and catch a bit of the fabric. Come up to the top in the same place. Working RL, whip twice into each large loop. Go into the fabric at the end of the row and come up again to start the next row, where the base of the gap formed in that row will lie.

» **8** Working LR, 1 x TB into each loop in the row. Go into the fabric at the end of the row and come up again to start the next row, where the ridge of DBH in that row will lie.

» **9** Working RL, [2 x DBH, 1 x DBH with picot, 2 x DBH into large loop]; repeat [--] to end and finish off the thread.

» **10** Thread 2mm (1/16in) silk ribbon onto a size 22 or larger tapestry (blunt-end) needle. Bring the needle up in the middle of the gap created by Row 7. Weave the ribbon over and under the bars. Take the needle to the back of the fabric. Come up in the middle of the gap created by Row 8. Weave the ribbon over and under the bars. Take the needle to the back of the fabric and end off the ribbon.

Please turn to page 93 to view stitch diagram.

[†] *Insertion lace.*

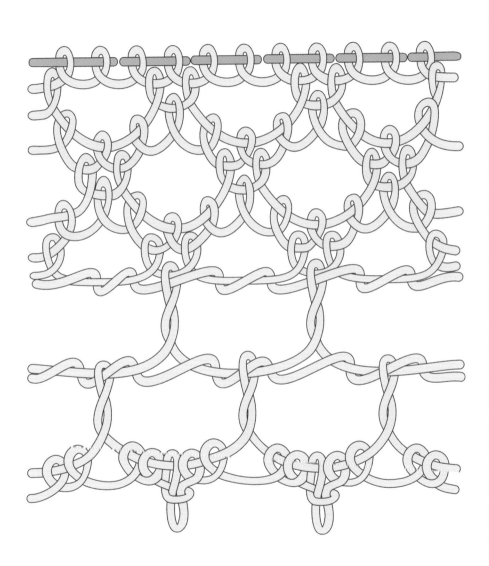

STITCH NO. 6[†]

PREPARATION	TOP ROW STITCH LENGTH
BS line along top, left and right edge	To accommodate 2 x DBH

» **1** Working LR, 2 x DBH into each BS. Go into the fabric at the end of the row and come up again to start the next row, where the ridge of DBH in that row will lie.

» **2** Working RL, [miss 2 loops, 1 x DBH into next loop, 1 x DBH into next loop]; repeat [--] to end. Go into the fabric at the end of the row and come up again to start the next row, where the ridge of DBH in that row will lie.

» **3** Working LR, [3 x DBH into large loop, 1 x DBH into small loop]; repeat [--] to end. Go into the fabric at the end of the row and come up again to start the next row, where the ridge of DBH in that row will lie.

» **4** Working RL, [miss 2 loops, 1 x DBH into next loop, 1 x DBH into next loop]; repeat [--] to end. Make sure that you go into the two loops in the middle of the group of three in the previous row. Go into the fabric at the end of the row and come up again to start the next row, where the ridge of DBH in that row will lie.

» **5** Working LR, 1 x DBH into each small loop. Go into the fabric, turn your work over and catch a bit of the fabric. Come up to the top in the same place. Working LR, whip twice into each large loop and once into any smaller loops at the beginning and end. Go into the fabric at the end of the row and come up again to start the next row, where the base of the gap formed in that row will lie.

» **6** Working LR, [2 x DBH into large loop, needle over and then under the loop that led up to the group, work a 2G+3 (see box on page 75),

move to next large loop]; repeat [--] to end. Go into the fabric, turn your work over and catch a bit of the fabric. Come up to the top in the same place. Working RL, whip once into each small loop and twice into each large loop. Go into the fabric at the end of the row and come up again to start the next row, where the base of the gap formed in that row will lie.

» **7** Working LR, 1 x DBH into each loop. Go into the fabric, turn your work over and catch a bit of the fabric. Come up to the top in the same place. Working LR, whip twice into each large loop and once into any smaller loops at the beginning and end. Go into the fabric at the end of the row and come up again to start the next row, where the base of the gap formed in that row will lie.

» **8** Working LR, [2 x DBH into large loop, needle over and then under the loop that led up to the group, work a 2G+3, move to next large loop]; repeat [--] to end. Go into the fabric at the end of the row and come up again to start the next row, where the ridge of DBH in that row will lie.

» **9** Working RL, [2 x DBH, 1 x DBH with picot, 2 x DBH into large loop]; repeat [--] to end and finish off the thread.

» **10** Thread 2mm (1/16in) silk ribbon onto a size 22 or larger tapestry (blunt-end) needle. Bring the needle up in the middle of the gap created by Row 6. Weave the ribbon over and under the bars. Take the needle to the back of the fabric. Come up in the middle of the gap created by Row 8. Weave the ribbon over and under the bars. Take the needle to the back of the fabric and end off the ribbon.

Please turn to page 97 to view stitch diagram.

[†] *Insertion lace.*

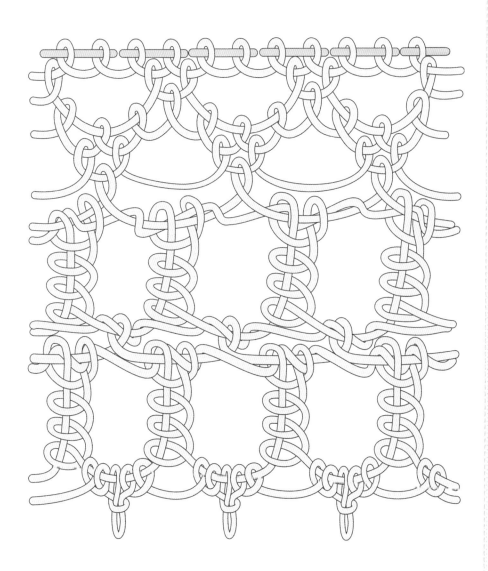

STITCH NO. 7[†]

PREPARATION	TOP ROW STITCH LENGTH
BS line along top, left and right edge	To accommodate 2 x DBH

» **1** Working LR, 2 x DBH into each BS. Go into the fabric at the end of the row and come up again to start the next row, where the ridge of DBH in that row will lie.

» **2** Working RL, [miss 2 loops, 1 x DBH into next loop, 1 x DBH into next loop]; repeat [--] to end. Go into the fabric at the end of the row and come up again to start the next row, where the ridge of DBH in that row will lie.

» **3** Working LR, [3 x DBH into large loop, 1 x DBH into small loop]; repeat [--] to end. Go into the fabric at the end of the row and come up again to start the next row, where the ridge of DBH in that row will lie.

» **4** Working RL, [miss 2 loops, 1 x DBH into next loop, 1 x DBH into next loop]; repeat [--] to end. Make sure that you go into the two loops in the middle of the group of three in the previous row.

» **5** Working LR, [3 x DBH into large loop, 1 x DBH into small loop]; repeat [--] to end. Go into the fabric at the end of the row and come up again to start the next row, where the ridge of DBH in that row will lie.

» **6** Working RL, [miss 2 loops, 1 x DBH into next loop, 1 x DBH into next loop]; repeat [--] to end. Make sure that you go into the two loops in the middle of the group of three in the previous row. Go into the fabric, turn your work over and catch a bit of the fabric. Come up to the top in the same place. Working LR, whip twice into each large loop. Go into the fabric at the end of the row and end off.

» **7** Work a TB (see box on page 51) into each loop in the row. When you reach the other side, go into the fabric, turn your work over and catch a bit of the fabric. Come up to the top in the same place. Working RL, whip twice into each large loop. Go into the fabric at the end of the row and come up again to start the next row, where the base of the gap formed in that row will lie.

» **8** Working LR, 1 x TB into each loop in the row. When you reach the other side, go into the fabric, turn your work over and catch a bit of the fabric. Come up to the top in the same place. Working RL, whip twice into each large loop. Go into the fabric at the end of the row and come up again to start the next row, where the base of the gap formed in that row will lie.

» **9** Working RL, 2 x DBH into each large loop. Go into the fabric at the end of the row and come up again to start the next row, where the ridge of DBH in that row will lie.

» **10** Working RL, [2 x DBH, 1 x DBH with picot, 2 x DBH into large loop]; repeat [--] to end and finish off the thread.

» **11** Thread 2mm (¹⁄₁₆in) silk ribbon onto a size 22 or larger tapestry (blunt-end) needle. Bring the needle up in the middle of the gap created by Row 6. Weave the ribbon over and under the bars. Take the needle to the back of the fabric. Come up in the middle of the gap created by Row 7. Weave the ribbon over and under the bars. Take the needle to the back of the fabric and end off the ribbon.

> **Please turn to page 101 to view stitch diagram.**

[†] *Insertion lace.*

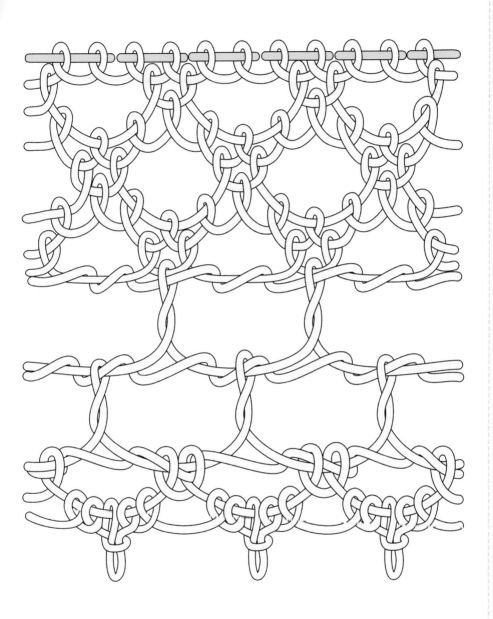

STITCH NO. 8[†]

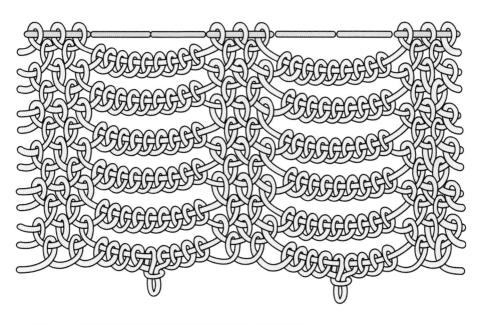

PREPARATION	TOP ROW STITCH LENGTH
BS line along top edge	To accommodate 3 x DBH

» **1** Working LR, [3 x DBH into BS, miss 2 BS]; repeat [--] to end. Go through the nearest BS down the right-hand side that is level with the ridge of the DBH in the row you have just worked. Snake down through the next BS.

» **2** *Working RL, [9 x DBH into large loop, 1 x DBH into small loop, 1 x DBH into small loop]; repeat [--] to end. Snake down to the next row.

» **3** Working LR, [1 x DBH into each small loop (i.e. 1 at the end of the group of 9 DBH in the previous row, 1 between the 2 DBH in the middle, and 1 at the beginning of the next group of 9]; repeat [--] to end. Snake down to the next row.*

» **4** Keep working the rows from * to * until you have a total of 5 repeats.

» **5** Working RL, [1 x DBH into each small loop (i.e. 1 at the end of the group of 9 DBH in the previous row, 1 between the 2 DBH in the middle, and 1 at the beginning of the next group of 9), 4 x DBH, 1 x DBH with picot, 4 x DBH into the large loop]; repeat [--] to end and finish off the thread.

STITCH NO. 9[†]

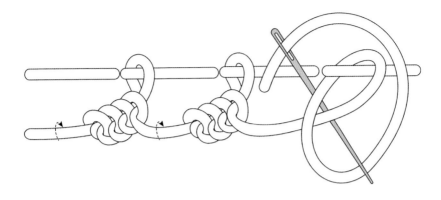

PREPARATION	TOP ROW STITCH LENGTH
BS line along top edge	To accommodate 2 x DBH

» **1** Miss the first BS, *go under the next one from the top down, catching the loop as you would for a DBH.

» **2** Go under what will now be a double loop, going over and catching the working thread to form a DBH at the bottom of the double loop.

» **3** Work a further 3 x DBH, working up the double loop to a total of 4 x DBH.*

» **4** Repeat from * to * until you have worked the buttonhole bar into the last BS.

» **5** Take the thread into the fabric about ½mm to 1mm away from the end of the BS. (This should make the last bar of the lace edging curl around towards the edge of the motif.)

» **6** It is unlikely that the lace scallops will sit nicely so, to this end, using a single strand of the same colour stranded cotton on a size 10 embroidery needle, couch a small stitch over the thread as indicated by the arrows in the diagram above. Pull the lace down, and also use your needle to place the buttonhole bar in a satisfactory position.

Note

Depending on where you place the edging, you may need to adjust the number of DBH on the double loop. For example, working on a sharp curve or going around a corner may mean that you need to make longer loops which would then require more DBH on those loops. You should adjust as necessary.

PICOT

» **1** Take the needle over and under the loop onto which the preceding DBH have been attached, catching the thread under a pin, which you have placed directly below the point where the ridge of the DBH lies.

» **2** Turning your work to the right, so that you are pulling the piece towards yourself, work a DBH over the threads that are held by the pin as indicated in the diagram. Then, making sure that the needle goes over the free thread, form a buttonhole stitch.

» **3** Turning your work upright again, continue straight into the next DBH that will be formed in the usual way over the loop.

Note
A picot can be made with additional DBH over the threads that are held by the pin, in which case you work those before continuing with the normal stitches that are formed over the loop at the top.

PICOT BAR EDGE

» **1** The bar can be worked with a total of either 3 or 5 stitches. Work a line of BS to accommodate the relevant number of stitches.

» **2** Bring the needle up out of the same hole where the BS started. Work a DBH over the BS (for a 3-stitch bar) or 2 x DBH (for a 5-stitch bar).

» **3** Referring to the instructions for making a picot (see page 107), work a single picot.

» **4** Work a DBH over the BS (for a 3-stitch bar) or 2 x DBH (for a 5-stitch bar) taking the needle back into the fabric where the BS ended.

» **5** Miss the next BS and continue by working bars on each alternate BS.

» **6** Return to the beginning and work bars on each of the unfilled BS.

THREE-ROW ARCH

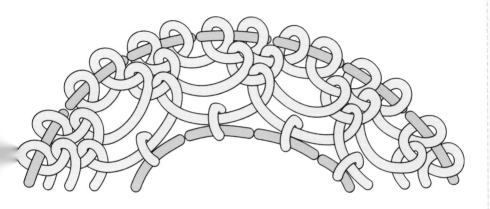

PREPARATION	TOP ROW STITCH LENGTH
BS line along top and bottom edges	To accommodate 2 x DBH

» **1** Working LR, 2 x DBH into each BS. Go into the fabric at the end of the row and come up again to start the next row, where the ridge of DBH in that row will lie.

» **2** Working RL, [1 x DBH each into two loops, miss a loop]; repeat [--] to end. Go into the fabric at the end of the row and come up again to start the next row, where the ridge of DBH in that row will lie.

» **3** Working LR, 1 x DBH into each small loop. Go into the fabric at the end of the row and come up again to start the next row, where the ridge of DBH in that row will lie.

» **4** Working RL, come up just below the bottom BS adjacent to the centre of the large loop in the third row of needle lace. Catch the loop and go into the fabric, tucking your needle under the BS and pulling firmly.

FOUR-ROW ARCH

PREPARATION	TOP ROW STITCH LENGTH
BS line along top and bottom edges	To accommodate 2 x DBH

» **1** Working LR, 2 x DBH into each BS. Go into the fabric at the end of the row and come up again to start the next row where the ridge of DBH in that row will lie.

» **2** Working RL, [1 x DBH each into three loops, miss a loop]; repeat [--] to end. Go into the fabric at the end of the row and come up again to start the next row, where the ridge of DBH in that row will lie.

» **3** Working LR, [1 x DBH each into two loops, miss a loop]; repeat [--] to end. Go into the fabric at the end of the row and come up again to start the next row, where the ridge of DBH in that row will lie.

» **4** Working RL, 1 x DBH into each small loop. Go into the fabric at the end of the row and come up again to start the next row, where the ridge of DBH in that row will lie.

» **5** Working LR, come up just below the bottom BS adjacent to the centre of the large loop in the third row of needle lace. Catch the loop and go into the fabric, tucking your needle under the BS and pulling firmly.

PADDED BUTTONHOLE
WITH BULLION KNOT PICOT

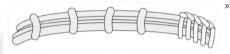

» **Option 1** Starting with a waste knot, work temporary, vertical, couching stitches over the shape, fanning the stitches as you go. Finish with a waste knot. Using the same thread, run long, horizontal stitches backwards and forwards (or in circles if you are doing a circle), weaving under the couching stitches. Keep filling the area until it is well padded. It is good to use a thicker thread – like Perle No. 8 for this padding.

» **Option 2** Using between 2–4 threads of stranded cotton, work rows of outline stitch backwards and forwards (or in circles if you are making a circle), until the shape is well padded.

» **1** Working with the thread advised for the buttonhole stitch, work 5 stitches over the padded area. Leave a gap of about a thread's width between each buttonhole stitch. Secure the last buttonhole stitch with a small couching stitch.

» **2** Come up between the 4th and 5th buttonhole stitches. Go down between the 3rd and 4th buttonhole stitches. Come back up between the 4th and 5th stitches, leaving your needle protruding from the fabric along with a loop of thread. Wrap around the needle eight times and pull the needle up through the wraps, tightening the thread to form a looped bullion knot. Do not take your needle through the fabric to complete the bullion stitch.

» **3** Continue straight into the 1st buttonhole stitch of the next group of 5, as illustrated. When you tighten that buttonhole stitch the bullion knot should pull around a bit, sitting almost at a right angle to the buttonhole stitch.

» **4** Working with a different colour or texture of thread, work straight stitches in the gaps that you left between the buttonhole stitches. Start at the base, burying the end of the stitch under the ridge of the buttonhole stitch.

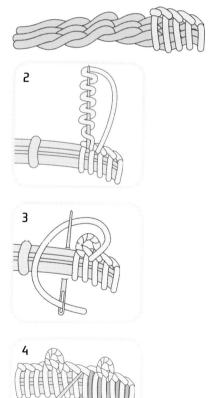

DAISY CENTRE

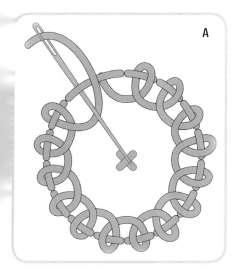

A

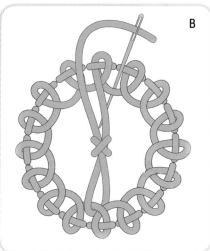

B

» **1** BS around the circle that forms the perimeter of the circle.
Note: *You will need to divide the number of BS by the number of petals that you would like the centre of the daisy to have, bearing in mind that you need to leave a space between each petal. For example, if you would like to have 8 petals, you need 16 or 24 BS. If you want to have 6 petals, you will need 12, 18 or 24 BS.*

» **2** Work a cross stitch in the middle of the circle.

» **3** Come out from under one of the BS and, referring to the diagram on the left (**A**), work a DBH into each BS until you get back to where you started.

» **4** When you work the last DBH in the circle, take the needle down through the cross stitch in the middle of the circle and pull through.

» **5** Go over and under the DBH loop in the circle that is exactly opposite the first loop. In the diagram, which consists of 16 BS and 16 loops, that is the 9th loop.

» **6** Go back through the cross stitch in the middle of the circle and pull through without making the loop too tight (**B**).

» **7** Go over and under the loop between the 1st and 2nd DBH in the circle, making sure that the needle goes under the thread that came from the circle and went into the cross stitch (see Step 4 above).

» **8** Pull through without making the loop too tight. Further along you will need to work DBH on these loops. They need to have a bit of give to allow you to do that.

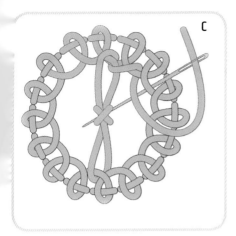

C

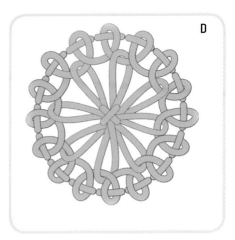

D

» **9** Whip the thread over the next loop, or as many loops as you need to.

» **10** Take your needle through the next loop and go through the cross stitch in the centre, repeating Steps 5 to 8 above (**C**).

» **11** Continue to add the double loops which create the petals of the centre daisy, whipping the loops that constitute the gaps in between, until you have filled the circle with the required number (**D**).

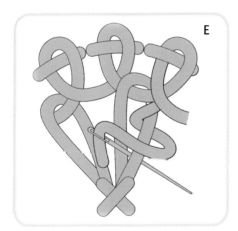

E

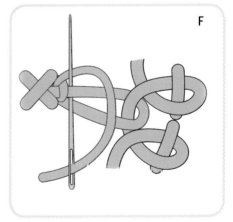

F

» **12** Whip down the far side of the last loop so that you take the working thread down to the centre of the circle (**E**).

» **13** Take the needle through the fabric to the back under the cross stitch.

» **14** Come up through the fabric under the cross stitch and work DBH over the thread of the loop. Work all the way around, going under the loop where it attaches to the outer loop space (**F**).

» **15** Go into the fabric under the cross stitch and come up for the next loop.

» **16** Complete all of the petals in the same way.

FILLERS

Once you have practised the stitches, and are well-versed in all of the needle lace techniques, you can start to play. Fillers, as depicted in the following two examples, are combinations of the numbered stitches that appear in the early pages of this guide (see pages 17–63). The combinations are endless and you should be able to make up your own by playing around with the techniques, adding ribbons, cords, beads and whatever else you can think up.

FILLER STITCH NO. 1

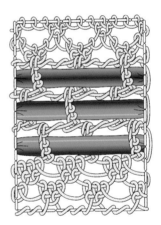

PREPARATION	TOP ROW STITCH LENGTH
BS all the way around the shape you wish to fill	To accommodate 2 x DBH

Please turn to page 123 to view full-size stitch diagram.

» **1** Working LR, 2 x DDH into each BS. Go through the nearest BS down the right-hand side that is level with the ridge of the DBH in the row you have just worked. Snake down through the next BS.

» **2** Working RL, [miss 2 loops, 1 x DBH into next loop, 1 x DBH into next loop]; repeat [--] to end. Snake down to the next row.

» **3** Working LR, [3 x DBH into large loop, 1 x DBH into small loop]; repeat [--] to end. Snake down to the next row.

» **4** Working RL, [miss 2 loops, 1 x DBH into next loop, 1 x DBH into next loop]; repeat [--] to end. Make sure that you go into the 2 loops in the middle of the group of 3 in the previous row.

» **5** Go into the fabric, turn your work over and catch a bit of the fabric. Come up to the top in the same place. Working RL, whip twice into each large loop and once into any smaller loops at the beginning and end. Snake down to start the next row, where the base of the gap formed in that row will lie.

» **6** Working RL, [2 x DBH into the small loop between the 2-DBH group in the previous row, needle over and then under the loop that leads up to the group, work a 2G+3 (see box on page 75)]; repeat [--] to end.

7 Go into the fabric, turn your work over and catch a bit of the fabric. Come up to the top in the same place. Working LR, whip once into each small loop and twice into each large loop. Snake down to start the next row, where the base of the gap formed in that row will lie.

8 Working the 2G + 3 into the large loops in the previous row, repeat Rows 6 and 7 as many times as you need to for the space that you are working in, bearing in mind that you will want to finish off with a repeat of Rows 3 and 4.

» **9** On the last repeat, do not whip back (Row 7).

» **10** Working into the large loops of the previous row, repeat Rows 3 and 4 until you have filled the space.

» **11** Finish off in the normal way, whipping through any visible BS, if necessary.

» **12** Thread 2mm (⅟₁₆in) silk ribbon onto a size 22 or larger tapestry (blunt-end) needle. Bring the needle up in the middle of the gap created by the buttonhole bars in the wide rows. Weave the ribbon over and under the bars.

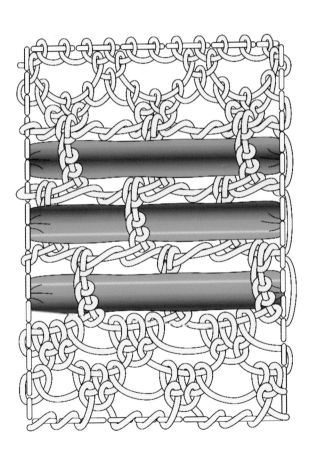

FILLER STITCH NO. 2

PREPARATION	TOP ROW STITCH LENGTH
BS all the way around the shape you wish to fill	To accommodate 2 x DBH

1 Working RL, come up through the fabric from under the BS, approximately opposite to where the ridge of the DBH will lie.

2 Work 1 x DBH into the first BS.

3 Miss the next BS and work 1 x DBH into the following BS, and every second BS thereafter, to the end of the row.

4 *Go into the fabric, placing your stitch under the BS on the left side, level with where the ridge of the DBH in the row lies.

» 5 Come up from under the BS at the point where you want to start the next row of DBH*. This sequence * to * is called the 'step down'.

» 6 Working LR, 2 x DBH into the loops between the DBH in the previous row.

» 7 Step down (see * to * on previous page).

» 8 Working RL, 1 x DBH into the loops that run between each pair of DBH in the previous row.

» 9 Step down (see * to * on previous page), this time leaving a larger space of about 3–4mm (approx. ⅛in) to accommodate the insertion row.

» 10 Working LR, 2 x DBH into the loops between the single DBH in the previous row.

» 11 Turn your work sideways; work 3 x DBH over the thread loop that leads up to the pair of stitches you have just worked.

» 12 Work 1 bar into each of the loops between the single DBH in the previous row.

» 13 Go into the fabric approximately level with where you started the row and step down (see * to * on previous page).

» 14 Work single DBH in the loops between the bars in the previous row.

» 15 Step down (see * to * on previous page).

» 16 Repeat Steps 6 to 15 as many times as you need to fill the centre of the petal.

» 17 Using the size 24 tapestry (blunt-end) needle, weave the 2mm (¹⁄₁₆in) ribbon over and under the buttonhole bars. Come up at the side, hiding the start under the backstitch and go in on the other side, hiding the end.

» 18 With the same needle, weave a strand of twisted cord; or, alternatively, work a metallic thread over and under the DBH in each of the rows of single stitches.

Please turn to page 127 to view stitch diagram.

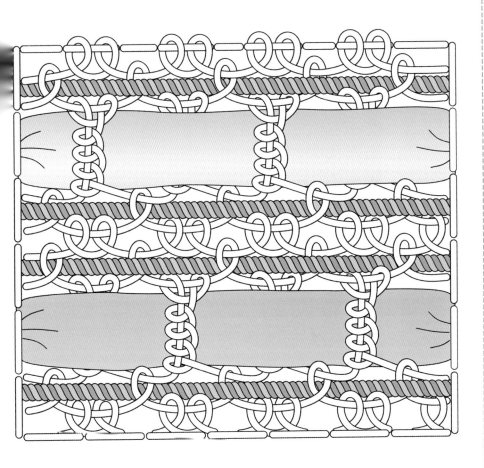